MW00947114

This book belongs to:

____

Made in the USA
Monee, IL
23 November 2024

71005329R00065